THE SLAVE MIND AND THE MASTER MIND

by Clyde King

*Published on the 400 year anniversary
of the arrival of the first enslaved Africans in 1619,
marking the beginning of U.S. slavery*

includes the following documents:
The Willie Lynch Letter
Dear Black Americans
We Charge Genocide (Excerpt)

Lynch

Eternal silence was the sentence
The only animation came
From the dance of the rising sun
The nocturnal crowd had devoured its prey
Retreating to its den
Its lustful appetite fed
Its terrorist act complete
What child?
Searching for daisies or butterflies
Or some other such simplicity
Would find these bitter
Strange fruits
And never be right again

TABLE OF CONTENTS

Page

THE WILLIE LYNCH LETTER

The content of this document was originally delivered as a speech by William "Willie" Lynch, an European slave owner and trainer, on the banks of the James River in Virginia in the year 1712. The psychological effects of the strategies used to maintain the African slave population nearly 300 years ago are still with us today.

Delivered by Willie Lynch

GENTLEMEN, I greet you here on the banks of the James River in the year of our Lord one thousand seven hundred and twelve. First, I shall thank you, the gentlemen of the Colony of Virginia for bringing me here. I am here to help you solve some of your problems with slaves. Your invitation reached me on my modest plantation in the West Indies where I have experimented with some of the newest and still the oldest methods for control of slaves. Ancient Rome would envy us if my program is implemented. As our boat sailed south on the James River, named for our Illustrious King, whose version of the Bible we cherish, I saw enough to know that your problem is not unique. While Rome used cords and wooden crosses for standing human bodies along its highways in great numbers, you are here using the tree and rope on occasion.

I caught the whiff of a dead slave hanging from a tree a couple miles back. You are not only losing valuable stock by hangings, you are having uprisings, slaves are running away, your crops are sometimes left in the fields too long for maximum profit, you suffer occasional fires, your animals are killed. Gentlemen, you know what your problems are? I do not need to elaborate. I am not here to enumerate your problems. However, I am here to introduce you to methods of solving them.

In my bag here, I have a full proof method for controlling your Black slaves. I guarantee every one of you that if installed correctly, it will control the slave for at least 300 years. My method is simple. Any member of your family or your overseer can use it.

I have outlined a number of differences among the slaves. I take these differences and make them bigger. I use fear, distrust, and envy for control purposes. These methods have worked on my modest plantation in the West Indies and it will work throughout the South. Take this simple little list of differences, and think about them.

On top of my list is Age, but it is there only because it starts with an "a". The second is Color or Shade. There is Intelligence, Plantation Size, Sex, Size of Plantations, Status of Plantation, Attitude of Owners, whether the slaves live in the Valley or on the Hills, East, West, North, South, Have Fine Hair, Course Hair, or is Tall or Short.

Now that you have a list of differences, I shall give you an outline of actions—but before that, I shall assure you that distrust is stronger than trust, and envy is stronger than adulation, respect or admiration.

The Negro slave after receiving this indoctrination shall carry on and will become self-fueling and self-generating for years, maybe thousands.

Don't forget, you must pitch the Old Negro Male versus the Young Negro Male and the Young Negro Male against the Old Negro Male. You must use the Dark Skin Slaves versus the Light Skin Slaves and the Light Skin Slaves versus the Dark Skin Slaves. You must use the Female versus the Male, and the Male versus the Female. You must also have your White Servants overseers distrust all Negros. But, it is necessary that your slaves trust and depend on us. They must love, respect and trust only us.

Gentlemen, these kits are your keys to control. Use them. Have your wives and children use them, never miss an opportunity. If used intensively for one year, the slaves themselves will remain perpetually distrustful. Thank you, gentlemen.

DEAR BLACK AMERICANS

The concepts and principles of the Willie Lynch Speech of 1712 are still at work as African Americans. This letter began circulating anonymously on the Internet since approximately 1999.

Dear Black Americans:

After all of these years and after all we have been through together, we think it's appropriate for us to show our gratitude for all you have done for us. We have chastised you, criticized you, punished you, and in some cases even apologized to you, but we have never formally nor publicly thanked you for your never-ending allegiance and support to our cause.

This is our open letter of thanks. We will always be in your debt for your labor. You built this country and were responsible for the great wealth we still enjoy today. Upon your backs, laden with the stripes we sometimes had to apply for disciplinary reasons, you carried our nation. We thank you for your diligence and your tenacity. Even when we refused to allow you to even walk in our shadows, you followed close behind believing that someday we would accept you and treat you like men and women.

We publicly acknowledge Black people for raising our children, attending to our sick, and preparing our meals while we were occupied with the trappings of the good life. Even during the time when we found pleasure in your women and enjoyment in seeing your men lynched, maimed and burned, some of you continued to watch over us and our belongings.

We simply cannot thank you enough. Your bravery on the battlefield, despite being classified as three-fifths of a man, was and still is outstanding. We often watched in awe as you went about your prescribed chores and assignments, sometimes laboring in the hot sun for 12 hours, to assist in realizing our dreams of wealth and good fortune. Now that we control at least 90 percent of all of the resources and wealth of this nation, we have Black people to thank the most. We can only think of the sacrifices you and your families made to make it all possible. You were there when it all began, and you are still with us today, protecting us from those Black people who have the temerity to speak out against our past transgressions.

Thank you for continuing to bring 95 percent of what you earn to our businesses. Thank you for buying our Hilfigers, Karans, Nikes, and all the other brands you so adore.

Your super-rich athletes, entertainers, intellectuals, and business persons (both legal and illegal) exchange most of their money for our cars, jewelry, homes, and clothing. What a windfall they have provided for use! The less fortunate among you spend all they have at our neighborhood stores, enabling us to open even more stores. Sure, they complain about us, but they never do anything to hurt us economically.

Allow us to thank you for not bogging yourself down with the business of doing business with your own people. We can taken care of that for you. You just keep doing business with us. It's safe that way. Besides, everything you need, we make anyway, even kente cloth. You just continue to dance, sing and distrust and hate one another. Tell you what. You don't need your own hotels. You can continue to stay in ours. You have no need for supermarkets when you can shop at ours 24 hours a day. Why should you even think about owning more banks? You have plenty now. And don't waste your energies trying to break into manufacturing. You worked hard enough in our fields.

Have yourself a good time, and this time we'll take care of you. It's the least we can do, considering all you've done for us. Heck, you deserve it, Black people. For all your labor, which created our wealth, for your resisting the messages of trouble-making Blacks like Washington, Delaney, Garvey, Bethune, Tubman, and Truth, for fighting and dying on our battlefields. We thank you. And we really thank you for not reading about the many Black warriors that participated in the development of our great country. We thank you for keeping it hidden from the younger generation. Thank you for not bringing such glorious deeds to their attention.

For allowing us to move into your neighborhoods, we will forever be grateful to you. For your unceasing desire to be near us and for hardly ever following through on your threats due to our lack of reciprocity and equity-- we thank you so much.

We also appreciate your acquiescence to our political agendas, for abdicating your own economic self-sufficiency, and for working so diligently for the economic well-being of our people. You are real troopers. And, even though the 13th, 14th, and 15th Amendments were written for you and many of your relatives died for the rights described therein, you did not resist when we changed those Black rights to civil rights and allowed virtually every other group to take advantage of them as well, even our own white women.

Black people, you are something else! Your dependence upon us to do the right thing is beyond our imagination, irrespective of what we do to you and the many promises we have made and broken. But this time we will make it right. We promise. Trust us. Relax. Have a party. We'll sell you everything you need. And when you die, we'll even bury you at a discount. How's that for gratitude?

Finally, the best part. You went beyond the pale and turned over your children to use for their education. With what we have taught them, it's likely they will continue in a mode similar to the ones you have followed for the past 45 years, since school desegregation.

When Willie Lynch walked on the banks of the James River in 1712 and said he would make you a slave for 300 years, little did he realize the trust of his prediction. Just 13 more years and his promise will come to fruition. But with two generations of your children having gone through our education systems, we can look forward to at least another 50 years of prosperity. Things could not be better. It's all because of you. For all you have done, we thank you from the bottom of our hearts, Black Americans. You're the best friends any group of people could ever have!

Sincerely,
–   All Other Americans

WE CHARGE GENOCIDE

The following is the introduction from We Charge Genocide, the 1951 book edition containing the complete historic petition presented by the Civil Rights Congress to the United Nations for relief from the crime of genocide by the United States government against the Negro people. It is proceeded by a reprint of Article II & III of the United Nations Convention on the Prevention and Punishment of the Crime of Genocide, adopted December 9, 1948.

ARTICLE II, CONVENTION ON THE PREVENTION AND PUNISHMENT OF THE CRIME OF GENOCIDE:
"In the present Convention, genocide means any of the following acts committed with intent to destroy, in whole or in part, a national, ethnical, racial or religious group, as such:
(a) Killing members of the group;
(b) Causing serious bodily or mental harm to members of the group;
(c) Deliberately inflicting on the group conditions of life calculated to bring about its physical destruction in whole or in part;
(d) Imposing measures intended to prevent births within the group;
(e) Forcibly transferring children of the group to another group."

ARTICLE III: "The following acts shall be punishable:
(a) Genocide;
(b) Conspiracy to commit genocide;
(c) Direct and public incitement to commit genocide;
(d) Attempt to commit genocide;
(e) Complicity in genocide."

We Charge Genocide
The Crime of Government Against the Negro
A Petition to the United Nations

Out of the inhuman Black ghettos of American cities, out of the cotton plantations of the South, comes this record of mass slayings on the basis of race, of lives deliberately warped and distorted by the willful creation of conditions making for premature death, poverty and disease. It s a record that calls aloud for condemnation, for an end to these terrible njustices that constitute a daily and every-increasing violation of the United Nations Convention on the Prevention and Punishment of the Crime of Genocide.

It is sometimes incorrectly thought that genocide means the complete and definitive destruction of a race of people. The Genocide Convention, however, adopted by General Assembly of the United Nations on December 9, 1948, defines genocide as any killings on the bases of race, or, in its specific words, as "killing members of the group." Any ntent to destroy, in whole or in part, a national, racial, ethnic or religious group is genocide, according to the Convention. Thus, the Convention states, "causing serious bodily or mental harm to members of the group" is genocide as well as "killing members of the group."

We maintain, therefore, that the oppressed Negro citizens of the United States, segregated, discriminated against and long the target of violence, suffer from genocide as the result of the consistent, conscious, unified policies of every branch of government.

The Civil Rights Congress has prepared and submits this petition to the General Assembly of the United Nations on behalf of the Negro people in the interest of peace and democracy, charging the government of the United States of America with violation of the Charter of the United Nations and the Convention on the Prevention and Punishment of the Crime of Genocide.

We believe that in issuing this document we are discharging an historic responsibility to the American people, as well as rendering a service of inestimable value to progressive mankind. We speak of the American people because millions of white Americans in the ranks of labor and middle class, and particularly those who live in the southern states and are often contemptuously called poor whites, are themselves suffering to an ever-greater degree from the consequences of the Jim Crow segregation policy of the government in its relations with Negro citizens. We speak of progressive mankind because a policy of discrimination at home must inevitably create racist commodities for export abroad—must inevitably tend toward war.

History has shown that the racist theory of government of the U.S.A. Is not the private affair of Americans, but the concern of mankind everywhere.

It is our hope, and we fervently believe that it was the hope and aspiration of every black American whose voice was silenced forever through premature death at the hands of racist-minded hooligans or Klan terrorists, that the truth recorded here will be made known to the world, that it will speak with a tongue of fire losing an unquenchable moral crusade, the universal response to which will sound the death knell of all racist theories.

We have scrupulously kept within the purview of the Convention on the Prevention and Punishment of the Crime of Genocide which is held to embrace those "acts committed with intent to destroy in whole or in part a national, ethnical, racial or religious group as such."

We particularly pray for the most careful reading of this material by those who have always regarded genocide as a term to be used only where the acts of terror evinced an intent to destroy a whole nation. We further submit that this Convention on Genocide is, by virtue of our avowed acceptance of the Covenant of the United Nations, an inseparable part of the law of the United States of America.

According to international law, and according to our own law, the Genocide Convention, as well as the provisions of the United Nations Charter, supersedes, negates and displaces all discriminatory racist law on the books of the United States and several states.

The Hitler crimes, of awful magnitude, beginning as they did against the heroic Jewish people, finally drenched the world in blood and left a record of maimed and tortured bodies and devastated areas such as mankind had never seen before. Justice Robert H. Jackson, who now sits upon the United States Supreme Court bench, described this holocaust to the world in the powerful language with which he opened the Nuremberg trials of the Nazi leaders. Every word he voiced against the monstrous Nazi beast applies with equal weight, we believe to those who are guilty of the crimes herein set forth.

Here we present the documented crimes of federal, state and municipal governments in the United States of America, the dominant nation in the United Nations, against 15,000,000 of its own nationals – the Negro people of the United States. These crimes are of the gravest concern to mankind. The General Assembly of the United Nations, by reason of the United Nations Charter and the Genocide Convention, itself is invested with power to receive this indictment and act on it.

The proof of this fact is its action upon the similar complaint of the Government of India against South Africa.

We call upon the United Nations to act and to call the Government of United States to account.

14

We believe that the test of the basic goals of a foreign policy is inherent in the manner in which a government treats its own nationals and is not to be found in the lofty platitudes that pervade so many treaties or constitutions. The essence lies not in the form, but rather, in the substance.

The Civil Right Congress is a defender of constitutional liberties, human rights, and of peace. It is the implacable enemy of every creed, philosophy, social system or way of life that denies democratic rights or one iota of human dignity to any human being because of color, creed, nationality or political belief.

We ask all men and women of good will to unite to realize the objectives set forth in the summary and prayer concluding this petition. We believe that this program can go far toward ending the threat of a third world war. We believe it can contribute to the establishment of a people's democracy on a universal scale.

But may we add as a final note that the Negro people desire equality of opportunity in this land where their contributions to the economic, political and social developments have been of splendid proportions, and in quality second to none. They will accept nothing less, and continued efforts to force them into the category of second class citizens through force and violence, through segregation, racist law and an institutionalized oppression, can only end in disaster for those responsible.

Respectfully submitted by the Civil Rights Congress as a service to the peoples of the world, and particularly to the lovers of peace and democracy in the United States of America.

– William L. Patterson

National Executive Secretary
Civil Rights Congress

THE SLAVE MIND AND THE MASTER MIND

In many countries we had chained the savage and starved him to death...in many countries we have burned the savage at the stake...we have hunted the savage and his little children and their mother with dogs and guns...in many countries we have taken the savage's land from him, and made him our slave, and lashed him every day, and broken his pride and made death his only friend, and overworked him till he dropped in his tracks...

– Mark Twain

From chattel slavery and colonization to economic dependency, African community's have endured a long history of challenges to our very survival. Though we have lost millions of lives during the African holocaust, we have managed to survive in great numbers into the new millennium. However, though many are with us physically in rank, many are absent mentally as their aspirations, perception, and self-identity is held captive by slavery-based behavior.

"Most psychiatrists and psychologists would agree that the Negro American suffers from a marred self-image, of varying degree, which critically affects his entire psychological being," stated Alvin F. Poussaint, a noted African-American psychologist and author of *Why Blacks Kill Blacks*. "It is also a well-documented fact that this negative self-concept leads to self-destructive attitudes and behavior that hinder the Negro's struggle toward full equality in American life."

To understand the dilemma of the African-American self concept we must go back to the bastardized birth of "the Negro" through the subjugation of the African during the holocaust of African enslavement. The purpose of reviewing this history and to speak in honest terms regarding the facts of this history is not to demonize the European, for he may have very well done an excellent job of doing that himself. This is not protest writing and his audience is not my aim. Its purpose is to create a brief historical picture for the African American to understand where slavery-based behavior, or the slave mind, originated. Once we understand its source, we can begin to consciously reverse its effects by developing a knowledge of self.

The Collective History

For nearly 300 years, men, women and children were torn away from their families, villages and their way of life only to be humiliated, chained and packed into vessels to endure months of a grueling transport under gunboat diplomacy across the Atlantic Ocean. Deeming the Native American's labor unsuitable, the African was imported to the so-called New World to toil at its many shorts under a highly organized and regulated European commerce system designed and managed by European aggression. From the sixteenth to the end of the eighteenth century the primary commodity of this commerce was indeed the trade of slaves—the African himself.

Categorized as less than human by the Euro-Americans, the African was treated as property on part with that of the European's cattle, as clearly documented in historical accounts and ledgers that inventoried Euro-American assets. As family ties were formed among the disenfranchised Africans, these new African families were many times broken up and scattered across auction blocks. The African male was emasculated and his character defamed. The African woman was sexually exploited, breed and her union with the African man reduced to the economics of the plantation system. For the slave, food, clothing, and shelter were provided by the slavers. The seeds of psychological dependency on Euro-American paternalism was being engrained.

When slavery was legislatively abolished in 1863, the African race in America was confronted with a hostile European dominated world of legalized segregation, terrorism, and lynching. If one wanted to research the psychological impact of a terrorized people, the African living under the racial caste system of America would be a perfect study.

The Slave Mind: Master or Servitude?

> *"as thou has believeth, so shall it be done unto thee..."*
>
> — King James Bible

17

What is the slave mind? In certain social circles within the African-American community to say that a person is "conscious" is to suggest that the person holds a high level of self-awareness and community-awareness. The content of this consciousness is a reflection upon the thoughts, feelings, images, dreams, body experiences and phenomenal experiences – beyond the body surface – of the person. To be conscious is to be wakeful. The options appear to either be awake, asleep or somewhere in between.

A person's personality is largely shaped by the character of his thoughts and the level of his consciousness. What is a thought? It is a energy. It is the mind's utterance of possibilities that is given form only through action. Everything that is in the physical world was first created in the world of the mind. Our very being is said to have been a thought in the mind of God.

It is an accepted truth that man is able to control the character of his thoughts. One would assume that through the exercise of judgment one would choose positive and empowering thoughts. Like a juke box, however – which is capable of only a limited selection-- what selection is your mind playing?

In viewing a landscape, certain elements automatically attract your attention. Our world, therefore, is very much what we choose to pay attention to. If, when visiting a maternity ward, your attention is automatically drawn to the crying, seemingly unhappy children, the scene will be for you a landscape of unhappy children. If, however, your attention is drawn to the children who are engaged in joyous activities, the landscape will be one of happy, youthful enjoyment. This leads us to voluntary attention. This is when the will chooses what and where its attention will lay, for attention can be directed by the will. By sheer force of will, many have withdrawn his attention from certain temptations and redirected it elsewhere. It seems that the way to develop and maintain a free will is to direct the attention and thought by means of the awakened Ego—which is the art of the Master Mind.

"The thinker comes first, then the thought, and then the form."
– Ernest Holmes

It is the master mind who has full control of his emotions, all thoughts are under the complete authority of his judgment and will. Within the slave mind, there is little or no exertion. The average man is a slave to his thoughts and feelings. The endless flow of the two leaves him in a constant state of reaction. He is prey to any thought or pulling that chances to enter his mind. The man is left a servant to outside influences and forces. On another level there are those who are partially influenced by outside forces. The thoughts are usually predicated upon a previous suggestion or statement, a so-called fact which was never verified or given little investigation.

The Bible reads: "as he thinks in his heart, so is he." Crash course on the thought. You are not your thoughts. There are thoughts behind every experience you have encountered in your life. A thing to note here is that thought takes form in action. The action of the will is based upon thoughts. Thought. Action. Form. If this is true, and it is, then being in control on your thoughts will place you in control of your experiences in life. The partners in each individual's thinking is directly responsible for the results in his life. We are capable of harming our body and healing our body with our thoughts. Your options, your possibilities, are limited only by your thinking.

Evaluate your circle of friends and associates. They are reflections of your thinking. Research has revealed that ones mental state is as infectious as a virus. We may literally catch another person's happiness as well as his sadness. This has great implications. An aware individual can resist the negative mental states of others through the development of his spiritual, mental and emotional selves. The development of these dynamic selves create a stability that guards against unwanted mental attitudes and attracts positive mental associations. It is impossible for a mentally healthy person to be happy and sad at the same time. Unhappiness is a habit. You choose which to entertain.

Much of our daily thinking is comprised of habitually reoccurring notions of "reality", or what we have come to believe as facts. Some of us are in the habit of talking about troubles, wallowing in self-pity and complaining about the conspiracy that is out to destroy us. This could be you or someone you have encountered. This individual is maintaining an unhappy state of mind by dwelling constantly in the halls of gloom and doom. You must begin to closely monitor your conversations and the conversations of others. Do others make a habit of taking you on their trip? Recognize and resist.

In the slave mind, the individual's uncontrolled will is effected by every passing desire or external suggestion that passes by him. This individual is not in control of his emotions, which makes his relationships unstable. His thoughts are easily swayed toward any suggestion that passes through the senses. He is a wrecked ship on a windy and turbulent sea. He makes few decisions for himself, though, again, he may actually believe that he makes all the decisions in his life. He is indeed subject to the stronger influence and wills of others.

The African American has developed a way of perceiving the world that makes him the mental slave to the will of others. This is in great part due to his history of direct human bondage under European enslavement. We have the unique distinction in U.S. society as being the only racial or ethnic group to be deliberately bred into a slavery caste system based on race. Seeking knowledge of self was forbidden among the slave population where the African's question to even learn to read was made an illegal act under U.S. Law. Thomas Paine's *Common Sense* was published in 1776. It would inspire European-Americans to fight a war against England for their freedom. In that same year, an African could have his hand chopped off for merely handling a book.

Your world, your reality is a reflection of your consciousness. Your awareness or lack thereof, and your attitude towards the world and community which you exist becomes a mirror. One of the slavery-based notions that has developed within the African-American collective unconscious is that of colorism. As the old African-American saying goes, "if you're Black step back, if you're Brown stick around, if you're White you're alright." Under this line of thinking, the more "white" something is the better – the "ideal" is that which is Europeanized. Many emulate White culture, attitudes, lifestyles, and predatory nature through a continuous quest for material possessions. Those who choose to play this game are so interlocked into their roles that they can not distinguish between the person they have been "playing" and their true selves. The real self is lost within the false self. If required, the false self will use any means necessary to maintain its existence. In dealing with such individuals you may find that they can become enraged when they are urged to examine their reality.

We were socialized to depend on others to think for us and to provide within society those things which the master mind would naturally provide for himself. These African Americans, whether consciously or unconsciously, see their only salvation through their god prototype of the white man. How many times have we heard an African American, some of which have been among our so-called leadership, offer us up for adoption through some such statement as "the problem is we need jobs in our community. If <u>they</u> would bring jobs to our community, we would not see the kind of problems we see in our community."

The Master Mind's keen radar immediately detects the psychic pains of slavery fueling such thinking and wonders why these individuals cannot develop opportunities for themselves. The highly observant scholar Carter Godwin Woodson in his classic work *The Mis-education of the Negro* observed the following:

> *It is most pathetic to see Negroes begging others for a chance as we have been doing recently. "Do not force us into starvation," we said. "Let us come into your stores and factories and do a part of what you are doing to profit by our trade." The Negro as a slave developed this fatal sort of dependency; and restricted mainly to menial service and drudgery during nominal freedom, he has not grown out of it.*

African Americans had not grown out of this thinking at Woodson's writing of this statement in 1933, nor have we grown out of it at the date of this writing in 2019. In 2002, the news media was reporting on the 10th anniversary of the L.A. Riots, which resulted from the video-taped beating of Rodney King by the LA. Police. The African American commentators on this anniversary were quick to stay in the reflections that the riots were not just a result of the Rodney King incident, but a result of the lack of jobs and opportunities for African Americans in the LA community where the riots broke out. One European American commentator on NPR posed a question to one of these African American commentators. "Was violently burning and looting their own community suppose to be an incentive to lure businesses into their community?"

In 2018, an Associated Press analysis of U.S. government data reported that Black workers who find jobs are in low-wage and less-prestigious fields such as food service or preparation or building maintenance and office work. According to the AP analysis, in comparison with White workers, Black workers were sorely underrepresented in high-salary jobs. This includes fields such as technology, engineering, architecture, life sciences and business. As reported by Woodson in 1933, Black workers remain restricted to menial service and drudgery work. This is the legacy of slavery and a failed Reconstruction. This is all being illustrated to show where we are mentally and to propose a self-healing of this destructive mental ailment. In other words, deliberately make your own chance.

The European American will set out to build a factory. He will gather resources from within his circle, making opportunities for those who are close to him. He knows he will need wage laborers to work in his factory to screw together his widgets, or oversee the screwing in of these widgets. As soon as his plan begins manifesting itself through his actions, the widget men and women will be drawn to him. The African American, many of which dare not entertained the thought of creating their own factories, will follow slave-based thinking and apply for a job at the European American owned factory.

He will work ten hours a day for slave wages, allow himself to be treated like a child, and will be happy to spend the next 25 years plugging in widgets. The African American will truly believe he has accomplished something by working in the White man's factory. He will walk around bragging about his pension, if such a thing is even offered, and will be encouraged by those within his community to believe that he has actually achieved something of notes. He is merely living at a survival level of existence. The true power, however, lies in the hands of the factory owner who will have become a respected Master Mind within his community.

The Master Mind

What is the Master Mind? He is the master of his mental faculties and is able to produce from this machinery works of the highest quality. Because he is master of himself, his powers naturally extend to his surrounding world. His supreme management of self leads others to readily accept his direction. That which is healthy to his happiness is divinely drawn to the master mind. He is a natural leader. The master mind reigns supreme in his environment. You are invited to become a Master Mind. It is up to you to accept the invitation. It is your choice and it is the first step on the road to becoming a Master Mind. Choose freedom or choose slavery.

Every African American will claim to know what is freedom. He will say that it is not to be a slave. It is not to be in physical bondage to another. Yet, freedom has greater meaning beyond freedom from physical restraint. Defining physical freedom is a relatively easy task Defining mental freedom requires deeper analysis. Mental freedom is being able to choose between two or more alternative courses of action. Take away the power of choice and freedom has also fled.

22

What is choice? Some will say choice is when "I can act as I wish." The key is that he can only act as he wishes. If his wishes are controlled, or have been defined, by entities outside of his own discriminate self, is it really freedom? If his wishes spring from his desires, then unless he controls his desires he does not control his wishes, but is in actuality being controlled by his desires. He is slave to his wishes, desires, feelings, passions (all coming from Lord-knows-where). He has no control over his thoughts and ideas which feed his desires, and which often create them. This is the main distinction between the Master Mind and the Slave Mind.

The undeveloped man, like a young child, is propelled to act freely upon each feeling or desire that passes through his mind. His restraint is determined to a great extent by his fear of consequences. An example of this is the person who is unable to restrain his desire for certain foods If a chocolate cake is placed in front of this person, not only will he eat one slice, but will later say that he could not help eating nearly the whole cake. He may have been restrained from eating the whole cake by the simple dynamics of physics. "If I eat one more bite I'll burst." It is easy to laugh at this exaggeration, but how many of us have been able to resist the temptations of today for the greater fruits of tomorrow.

There have been numerous African-American Master Minds despite the challenges presented by their environments. We can look at someone like Benjamin Banneker (1731-1806). Banneker was an African American who was a mathematician, astronomer, almanac editor, and an inventor. It is known that he was part of the team which laid the boundaries for the present city of Washington D.C. But what is even more impressive was that he was an African man during slavery influencing the White elite through the power of his mental faculties.

If the goal is freedom, then by reducing the "things" we need to the true essentials, the freer we will be emotionally, spiritually, economically, and socially. The fewer the needs, the more independent we will become. The more you think you need, the more of a slave you are inclined to be in your quest to feed the slave mind's appetite for material possessions, psychological dependency upon other groups, etc. You must learn to distinguish the difference between a desire and a need. You must work on freeing yourself from slave mind thinking. Chinweizu, African poet and scholar, speaks of the importance of the re-establishment of power in our collection struggle when he states:

We, like many other peoples of the world, lost our dignity when we lost our power. And some of our fellow losers who have recovered their dignity today have so only by first recovering their power. Those who want dignity must pay for it in its proper currency--Power"

Much of our collective power lies in how we raise the next generation. Will they continue the legacy of the slave mind or will they be Master Minds? Teach our children early about who we are as a people spanning the course of human history. Develop the inner life of a child.

Dr. Carol Leal in her monograph entitled *Successful Parenting in the Black Community*, lays out the objectives of the optimal development of the next generation.

The goal of the Black Parent should be to promote physically adept individuals who are functioning optimally in accordance with their stage of psycho-genetic, psycho-social, emotional, adoptive and temperamental development and in keeping with the capacities of their biological integrity and cognitive potential.

Instill a strong sense of pride in our children by engaging them in a variety of hobbies to stimulate their minds. Teach them about their thoughts. Teach them about the unlimited potential that their existence in the universe holds. Give them choices. It is the African-American's parents duty to ensure that the child is provided quality education that not only imparts information but encourages them to think and do for themselves. The purpose of our education should not be for the service of others, but service to our collective power. Franz Fanon tell us in *Wretched of the Earth* that "each generation must, out of relative obscurity, discover its mission, fulfill it, or betray it.

Which form comes first: that which reflects or that which is reflected? Your world, your reality is a reflection of your consciousness. Your awareness or lack thereof, and your attitude towards the world and community in which you exist becomes a mirror. Expand your self awareness, expand your thinking and expand your enjoyment of life.

SUGGESTED READING LIST

- *The New Jim Crow: Mass Incarceration in the Age of Colorblindness* by Michelle Alexander and Cornel West
- *Before the Mayflower: A History of the Negro in America 1619-1964* by Lerone Bennett, Jr.
- *Discourse of Colonialism* by Aimé Césaire
- *Christopher Columbus and the Afrikan Holocaust: Slavery and the Rise of European Capitalism* by John Henrik Clarke
- *The African Origin of Civilization: Myth or Reality* by Cheikh Anta Diop and Mercer Cook
- *Black Skin White Masks* by Franz Fanon
- *Message to the People: The Course of African Philosophy* by Marcus Garvey
- *Unchained Memories: Readings from the Slave Narratives* forward by Henry Louis Gates, Jr., introduction by Spencer Crew
- *Stolen Legacy* by George James
- *We Charge Genocide* by William L. Patterson
- *The Isis Papers: The Keys to Colors* by Dr. Frances Cress Welsing
- *The Destruction of Black Civilization* by Dr. Chancellor Williams
- *The Mis-education of the Negro* by Carter Godwin Woodson

www.ingramcontent.com/pod-product-compliance
Lightning Source LLC
Chambersburg PA
CBHW051409280526
45784CB00007B/3159